About Skill Builders
Grammar
Grade 3

Welcome to Skill Builders *Grammar* for third grade. This book is designed to improve children's grammar skills through focused practice. This full-color workbook contains grade-level-appropriate activities based on national standards to help ensure that children master basic skills before progressing.

More than 70 pages of activities cover essential grammar skills, such as parts of speech, capitalization, punctuation, and usage. The book's colorful, inviting format, easy-to-follow directions, and clear examples help build children's confidence and make grammar more accessible and enjoyable.

The Skill Builders series offers workbooks that are perfect for keeping skills sharp during the school year or preparing for the next grade.

Credits:

Content Editors: Joyce Cockson and Elizabeth Swenson
Copy Editor: Beatrice Allen
Layout and Cover Design: Nick Greenwood

www.carsondellosa.com
Carson-Dellosa Publishing LLC
Greensboro, North Carolina

D0869135

Printed in the USA • All rights reserved.
1 2 3 4 5 HPS 15 14 13 12 11

ISBN 978-1-936023-20-2
335101151

Table of Contents

Nouns

Circle each noun. The number in parentheses tells the number of nouns in each sentence.

A **noun** is a word that names a person, place, or thing.

Examples:	**Person**	girl, Beth
	Place	library, Chicago, Illinois
	Thing	book, Rosetta Stone

1. Raccoons are animals that usually hunt for food at night. (4)

2. In North America, there are several kinds of raccoons. (3)

3. A raccoon usually weighs 4 to 23 pounds (1.8 to 10.4 kilograms). (3)

4. A raccoon usually has five to seven dark rings on its tail and a black mask on its face. (5)

5. Raccoons like swampy areas or woods near water. (4)

Common Nouns

Circle each common noun. The number in parentheses tells the number of common nouns in each sentence.

> A **common noun** names a general person, place, or thing.
>
> Example: The (boy) saw a (mouse) near the (road).

1. Mice are small rodents with sharp teeth. (3)

2. Mice have pointed noses and slender bodies. (3)

3. Some mice live in grassy or marshy areas. (2)

4. Mice can live on the plains or in the deserts. (3)

5. Some mice eat insects. (2)

6. I read a book about mice and other rodents. (3)

7. The pygmy mouse is the smallest mouse in the world. (3)

8. The most common mouse lives around the house. (2)

Proper Nouns

Circle each proper noun.

A **proper noun** names a specific person, place, or thing.
A proper noun begins with a capital letter. Each word in a
proper noun begins with a capital letter.

Example: Mrs. Ling took Andrew to see the Great Barrier
            Reef in Australia.

president   Monday   park

Oak Street   Katherine   George Washington

Mr. Toma   state   Piedmont Park

South Dakota   street   Roberto

Plural Nouns

Write the plural form of each noun.

A **singular noun** names only one person, place, or thing. A **plural noun** names more than one person, place, or thing.

Add -s to form most plural nouns. Add -es if a noun ends in -s, -sh, -ch, or -x.

Examples:

Singular	Plural
brother	brothers
bunch	bunches

Singular   **Plural**

1. hat   _____

2. beach   _____

3. coat   _____

4. box   _____

5. trunk   _____

Singular Possessive Nouns

Rewrite each group of words using a possessive noun.

A **singular possessive noun** shows that a person, place, or thing owns or has something.

Add an apostrophe (') and –s to a singular noun to show ownership.

Example: the jacket of the boy   the **boy's** jacket

1. the teacher of the class

   _____

2. the tail of the dog

   _____

3. the bark of the tree

   _____

4. the skirt of the girl

   _____

5. the book of the student

   _____

Plural Possessive Nouns

Rewrite each underlined noun as a plural possessive noun.

A **plural possessive noun** shows that more than one person, place, or thing owns or has something. Add an apostrophe (') at the end of plural nouns to show ownership.

Example: **students'** books

1.   The two <u>babies</u> gifts are very cute.

    _____

2.   Both of the <u>students</u> grades are good.

    _____

3.   All of the <u>ships</u> flags were the same.

    _____

4.   My <u>grandparents</u> attic is neat.

    _____

5.   The three <u>dogs</u> tails are wagging.

    _____

Review: Nouns

Underline each noun. Capitalize each proper noun.

Mammoth Cave National Park

mammoth cave is the world's longest known cave system. mammoth cave is also part of mammoth cave national park. The park is located in central kentucky. The green river and the nolin river flow through the park. This national park was created in 1941.

mammoth cave is sometimes called one of the wonders of the western hemisphere. The cave is located on a ridge made mainly of limestone. There are 14 miles (22.5 kilometers) of walkways through which visitors can be guided. The cave has five levels. The lowest level is 360 feet (110 meters) below the surface. There are many rocks in the cave that have interesting colors and shapes.

Several lakes and rivers can be found in the cave. The largest river, echo river, varies in width from 20 to 60 feet (6–18 meters) and from 5 to 25 feet (1.5–7.6 meters) in depth. Strange eyeless fish live in echo river. They are about 3 inches (7.6 centimeters) long and are colorless. There are many types of blind creatures that live in mammoth cave.

Pronouns

Circle each pronoun.

A **pronoun** is a word that takes the place of one or more nouns.

Singular	**Plural**
I, me	we, us
you	you
he, him, she, her, it	they, them

1. Tomorrow, we are going to the skating rink.

2. Amy and I love to ice skate.

3. You should try skating. It is fun.

4. They will join us later at the rink.

5. We will meet him later.

6. Follow me to the ice.

7. I want to skate like her. She is very good.

8. He will wait for them to finish.

Pronouns

Circle the pronouns that can take the place of each noun. Some nouns will have more than one answer.

Nouns	Pronouns		
1. Ava	she	he	her
2. Nicholas	it	him	he
3. forks	them	it	they
4. doll	her	them	it
5. Boston	he	it	she
6. sister	you	she	her
7. friends	they	them	it
8. desk	it	he	her
9. Dr. Ross	she	he	her
10. trees	him	they	them

Subject Pronouns

Circle each subject pronoun.

A **subject pronoun** is the subject of a sentence. The subject tells what or whom the sentence is about.

Singular Subject Pronouns		Plural Subject Pronouns	
I	she	we	they
you	it	you	
he			

1. I saw a squirrel run across the yard and up a tree.

2. It lives in the oak tree next door in my neighbor's yard.

3. We enjoy watching the squirrels chase each other.

4. They eat seeds, nuts, berries, and insects.

5. You can come watch the squirrels tomorrow.

6. Does he have a squirrel feeder near the house?

7. She does not like watching the squirrels.

8. You and I should read a book about squirrel habitats.

Object Pronouns

Circle the correct object pronoun to complete each sentence.

An **object pronoun** comes after an action verb or after words such as *to*, *of*, *for*, *with*, or *at*. An object pronoun tells who or what receives the action.

Examples: Jeff went to the park with (him).
(singular object pronoun)
Jamar threw the ball to (us).
(plural object pronoun)

Singular Object Pronouns

me	her	
you	it	
him		

Plural Object Pronouns

us
them

1.   The chef showed (they, them) how to make the cake.

2.   Please give the new book to (me, I).

3.   Marcus walked with (he, him) to school.

4.   Anna's dog ran quickly to greet (she, her).

5.   We wanted to give (them, they) one of the puppies.

Possessive Pronouns

Circle the correct possessive pronoun to complete each sentence.

A **possessive pronoun** shows ownership and takes the place of a possessive noun.

Example: Emma and Will's project is due tomorrow.
            (Their) project is due tomorrow.

Singular Possessive Pronouns		Plural Possessive Pronouns	
my	hers	our	yours
mine	his	ours	their
yours	its	your	theirs
her			

1.   (My, She, They) cousin is coming for a visit.

2.   Is that (he, it, your) silver car in the driveway?

3.   Renee thought it was (she, hers, our) suitcase.

4.   Which one of these sweaters is (yours, I, you)?

5.   (Their, I, They) team was winning the game.

Review: Pronouns

Circle the correct pronoun to complete each sentence.

1. Let _____ take his turn.

   A. it   B. his

   C. him   D. he

2. Where did you say that _____ was located?

   A. it   B. his

   C. him   D. they

3. Ask _____ sister to join our game.

   A. it   B. her

   C. him   D. he

4. Did you know that _____ is playing too?

   A. it   B. his

   C. him   D. she

5. _____ wanted us to join the team.

   A. They   B. Them

   C. We   D. Us

Verbs

Circle each verb.

An **action verb** is a word that tells what a person or thing is doing or has done.

Example: Melanie (borrowed) my new pencil.

1. Four to six horses pulled each covered wagon.

2. The American settlers built the first covered wagons in Conestoga, Pennsylvania.

3. The wagons carried heavy loads across the prairies.

4. Large wheels help the wagon over ruts and through mud on the prairie roads.

5. White canvas coverings protect the wagons against bad weather.

6. The new display at the museum shows a Conestoga wagon model.

Action Verbs

Circle each action verb.

An **action verb** is a word that shows action. An action verb tells what a person or thing is doing.

Example: The children (run), (jump), and (play).

1. Robots do tasks with instructions.

2. Workers control the robots through stored instructions.

3. Robots search the seafloor for new discoveries.

4. Some robots explore other planets.

5. Workers give some robots special equipment.

6. Rescue robots find people and save lives.

7. Special tasks need robots with specific abilities.

8. Police robots climb, grab, and record video.

Linking Verbs

Circle each linking verb.

A **linking verb** links the subject to the rest of the sentence. A linking verb does not show action. Many linking verbs are states of the verb "to be."

Examples: They (are) on a science field trip.

She (is) my favorite teacher.

Singular Linking Verbs		Plural Linking Verbs
am	is	are
are	was	were
were		

1.   I am a scientist who studies insects.

2.   Insects are the most plentiful creatures on Earth.

3.   Monarch butterflies are migrating butterflies.

4.   A bee is a flying insect that can sting.

5.   A moth is different from a butterfly.

Helping Verbs

Circle each helping verb.

A **helping verb** helps the main verb show an action. When a main verb has a helping verb, the main verb sometimes adds *-ing*.

Example: Maria (was) cleaning her room when I called.

1.   Monique is enjoying the art class.

2.   Nathan and I are learning about painting.

3.   Chang wishes that he could take the art class.

4.   Miss Harrison has taught art for 12 years.

5.   Many of my friends will take the art class.

6.   Last year, art class had included two projects.

7.   Art should involve getting messy.

8.   My painting will hang on the wall at home.

Present-Tense Verbs

Circle the present-tense verb in parentheses to complete each sentence.

> A **present-tense verb** expresses an action that is happening now.
>
> Examples: A spider (spins) silk to build a web.
>
> Spiders (spin) silk to build webs.

1. Spiders (use, used) their webs to catch insects for food.

2. Some spiders do not (make, made) webs.

3. All spiders (had, have) eight legs.

4. The bolas spider (swung, swings) a line of web at an insect.

5. This spider (trapped, traps) the insect on the sticky ball.

6. Webs (were, are) different for each type of spider.

7. Morning dew (left, leaves) water droplets on the webs.

8. Gardens (need, needed) spiders to stay healthy.

Past-Tense Verbs

Use the correct ending to write the past-tense form of each verb.

A **past-tense verb** expresses an action that has already happened.

Examples:	**Present Tense**		**Past Tense**
	talk	→	talk**ed**
	hurry	→	hurr**ied**
	taste	→	tast**ed**
	wag	→	wagg**ed**

1. Marco Polo _____ in Asia in the late
    1200s.   (travel)

2. He probably _____ at the city of
    Shangdu in 1275.   (arrive)

3. Polo _____ through China for about
    17 years.   (roam)

4. He _____ home around 1292.
           (sail)

5. People _____ Polo's travels through
    Asia.   (study)

Future-Tense Verbs

Write the correct future-tense form of each verb.

A **future-tense verb** expresses an action that will happen. A future tense verb uses the helping verb *will*.

Example: The dogs **will play** in the backyard.

1. Owen _____ a report about Thomas Edison.
   (write)

2. José _____ for his math test.
   (study)

3. Bryan and Mario _____ in the concert.
   (sing)

4. The dog _____ the bone for dinner.
   (enjoy)

5. The class _____ the next field trip.
   (plan)

6. Your cat _____ on the bookshelf.
   (jump)

Irregular Verbs

Circle the correct irregular verb in parentheses to complete each sentence.

An **irregular verb** has a different spelling when used in the past tense or with a helping verb.

Present	Past	Past with a Helping Verb
do	did	had done
run	ran	had run
go	went	had gone
come	came	had come
see	saw	had seen

1. The tennis player (run, ran) up and down the court.

2. We (seen, saw) three professional tennis players.

3. They had (come, came) to play in the tournament.

4. The player (go, went) to receive her trophy.

5. I have (do, done) very well this year.

Irregular Verbs

Circle the correct irregular verb to complete each sentence.

An **irregular verb** has a different spelling when used in the past tense or with a helping verb.

Present	Past	Past with a Helping Verb
begin	began	had begun
eat	ate	had eaten
give	gave	had given
sing	sang	had sung
take	took	had taken

1. Robins have (eaten, eat) worms for their meals.

2. The robin (sing, sang) outside my window this morning.

3. Tyrone had (gave, given) the bird a bath.

4. The squirrels (taken, took) the bird food from the feeder.

5. He (begin, began) to care for his brother's bird.

Contractions with *Not*

Write the contraction for each word or pair of words.

A **contraction** is the shortened form of two words. An apostrophe (') takes the place of any letters that are left out.

Example: do + not → don't

1. cannot

    _____

2. have not

    _____

3. could not

    _____

4. were not

    _____

5. does not

    _____

6. should not

    _____

7. did not

    _____

8. would not

    _____

Pronouns in Contractions

Write the contraction for each pair of words.

A **contraction** is the combined form of two words. A contraction can combine a pronoun with a verb. An apostrophe (') is used in place of the letter or letters that are left out.

Example: I + have → I've

1. you had

2. he has

3. it has

4. she would

5. I am

6. you are

7. we will

8. they have

9. she is

10. I will

Review: Verbs

Circle the correct verb form to complete each sentence.

1. The baseball players (play, played) in the park last night.

2. The fans (cheer, cheered) when the player hit a home run.

3. We (saw, seen) both of these teams play last season.

4. That train (stop, stops) at this station at 1:00 P.M. every day.

5. I had (watch, watched) the train pull into the station.

6. Carlos (begin, began) to collect trains when he was five years old.

7. I (have, has) enjoyed looking at your artwork.

8. There (wasn't, weren't) much warning before the storm.

Review: Verbs

Circle the correct sentence in each group.

1. A. Josh gone to see his uncle.

    B. His uncle weren't at home.

    C. Then, Josh walked to the corner store.

    D. After going to the store, he were walking home.

2. A. Shane's car had a flat tire.

    B. His sister has took it to the repair shop.

    C. The man at the repair shop telled her he could fix it.

    D. Shane were wondering how much it would cost.

3. A. We riding our bicycles to the library.

    B. Our teacher assign us a report for Monday.

    C. The librarian helping us with the research.

    D. We were able to finish our report on time.

4. A. Mariah go to the library to find a book.

    B. My mother singed in the program.

    C. Mark's train jumped the track in his room.

    D. Didn't you walked to school today?

Review: Nouns, Pronouns, and Verbs

Write each word or phrase next to the correct part of speech. Each choice is used only once.

walk	me	can't	our
raccoon	made	Paris	he'd
they	will study	stories	is

1. Plural noun _____

2. Pronoun in contraction _____

3. Possessive pronoun _____

4. Past-tense verb _____

5. Common noun _____

6. Subject pronoun _____

7. Future-tense verb _____

8. Object pronoun _____

9. Action verb _____

10. Proper noun _____

11. Linking verb _____

12. Contraction _____

Adjectives

Draw an arrow from each underlined adjective to the noun that it describes.

An **adjective** is a word that describes a noun. An adjective tells what kind or how many.

Example: We rode in a colorful balloon.

1.   Hot air balloons can carry heavy loads.

2.   Large ropes are used just before landing.

3.   A strong person on the ground grabs the ropes.

4.   Two brave papermakers began experimenting with balloons in the 1700s.

5.   They started by filling paper bags with smoke.

Adjectives

Write three adjectives to describe each noun.

flowers

hat

_____

_____

_____

_____

_____

_____

dog

hands

_____

_____

_____

_____

_____

_____

building

car

_____

_____

_____

_____

_____

_____

Adjectives—How Many?

Circle each adjective that tells how many.

An **adjective** is a word that describes a noun. Some adjectives tell how many.

Example: (Several) students had pencils.

1. Many doctors are located in this building.

2. After the game, most students walked home.

3. Our vacation lasted several days.

4. On our vacation, we passed through many towns.

5. There are 100 grapes in that bin.

6. A few movies are showing tonight.

7. There are six eggs in that carton.

8. You have some crayons in the box.

Adjectives—What Kind?

Circle the adjective that describes each underlined noun.

An **adjective** is a word that describes a noun. Some adjectives tell what kind.

Example: We saw (little) prairie dogs.

1.   Prairie dogs live in underground <u>burrows</u>.

2.   A prairie dog puts dried <u>plants</u> in its nest.

3.   A prairie dog gives birth to a litter of tiny <u>pups</u>.

4.   The prairie dog is a good <u>mother</u>.

5.   The brave <u>pups</u> are ready to leave the nest after six weeks.

6.   The average <u>prairie dog</u> is the size of a rabbit.

7.   Friendly <u>prairie dogs</u> greet each other with a kiss.

8.   Black-tailed prairie dogs are a famous <u>species</u>.

Articles *A, An,* and *The*

Circle each article. Underline the noun following each article.

The words *a, an,* and *the* are special adjectives called **articles**.

A singular noun that begins with a consonant uses the article *a*.

Example: (a) chair

A singular noun that begins with a vowel or with a silent letter *h* uses the article *an*.

Examples: (an) apple
             (an) hour

A noun that names a particular person, place, or thing uses the article *the*. A plural noun always uses the article *the*.

Examples: (the) game
             (the) movies

1. Our dog sleeps in a doghouse.

2. The movie made us laugh.

3. I carried an umbrella in the rain.

4. Our boat had a leak.

5. Earth revolves around the sun.

Adjectives—Comparatives

Write the correct comparative adjective to complete each sentence.

A **comparative adjective** compares two nouns. Most adjectives add -*er* to the end of the word to compare two nouns.

Example: This tree is **taller** than that tree.

1. Australia is a _____ continent than Asia.
    (small)

2. My classroom is _____ than your classroom.
    (cold)

3. This blanket is_____ than the blanket on my bed.
    (soft)

4. A yardstick is_____ than a ruler.
    (long)

5. The ocean is _____ than a swimming pool.
    (deep)

Adjectives–Superlatives

Write the correct superlative adjective to complete each sentence.

A **superlative adjective** compares three or more nouns.
Most adjectives add -*est* to the end of the word to compare three or more nouns.

Example: That dog has the **shortest** tail of all.

1. Ashley's hair is the _____ of all of the girls in our class.   (long)

2. That is the _____ movie at the theater.   (short)

3. That horse is the_____ in the barn.   (tall)

4. This wood is the_____ of all of the trees in the forest.   (hard)

5. Your rope is the _____ in the entire group.   (long)

Adverbs

Circle each adverb.

An **adverb** is a word that describes or tells more about a verb or an adjective. An adverb can tell how an action happens. Adverbs often end in –*ly*.

Example: The students sat (quietly).

1.   Three kittens happily played with the ball of yarn.

2.   Mrs. Lee carefully pulled the weeds in the garden.

3.   Ming and Lisa were walking quickly to the store.

4.   Did you see the horse gracefully jump the fence?

5.   Suddenly, the dog began to bark at the bird in the tree.

6.   Why are you talking quietly?

7.   She waited patiently for her flight.

8.   We eagerly watched the baker for the fresh muffins.

Adverbs

Insert adverbs from the word bank to make the paragraph more interesting. Use the insert symbol (^).

carefully	eagerly	extremely
finally	later	next
rapidly	slowly	soon
suddenly	then	very

The Train Trip

I packed for our trip. My mother said that we were leaving

today. We boarded the train. I was excited about our trip. We

walked down the aisle to our seats. The train began to move. It

travelled down the tracks. We were on our way. The ride ended.

We left the train.

Adverbs—*When?*

Circle each adverb.

An **adverb** is a word that describes or tells more about a verb or an adjective. An adverb can tell when an action happens.

Example: We will go to the store (tomorrow).

1. Myla is **always** on time for school.

2. **Yesterday**, I walked to the grocery store with my sister.

3. The teacher **often** surprises us with treats.

4. Amber is coming to my house **today** after school.

5. **Now**, we are going to begin our history project.

6. Dad should have dinner ready **soon**.

7. We **usually** go for a walk at sunset.

8. You wake up **early** in the morning.

Adverbs—*Where?*

Circle each adverb.

An **adverb** is a word that describes or tells more about a verb or an adjective. An adverb can tell where an action happens.

Example: The music played (inside).

1. The coach said that we should run outside.

2. Some of the team members thought that we ran far.

3. The practice equipment is sitting there.

4. Nadia told us to kick the ball forward.

5. The mother bear walked close to her cubs.

6. Cory's family lives near my house.

7. We drove past the store.

8. The dog jumped through the hoop.

Review: Adverbs

Circle each adverb. Underline the verb that each adverb describes.

1. Jayla closes the book quickly.

2. Thad often plays in the park.

3. Miranda will watch a movie tonight.

4. Zack worked quietly on his model.

5. Leo ran on the path yesterday.

6. Pete and Sarah flew to their grandmother's city today.

7. Wesley will miss his game tomorrow.

8. Tracy mixed the ingredients carefully.

9. Rick will eat strawberries later.

10. Alexis always stops to pick flowers.

Adjective or Adverb?

Write *ADJ* if the underlined word is an adjective. Write *ADV* if the underlined word is an adverb.

An **adjective** describes a noun. Adjectives tell which one, how many, or what kind.

An **adverb** describes a verb or an adjective. Adverbs tell how, when, or where something happens.

1. _____ Three huge fish swam <u>quickly</u> through the water.

2. _____ <u>Many</u> people work in that building.

3. _____ Those new shoes fit <u>really</u> well.

4. _____ Malia and her brother boarded the <u>beautiful</u> boat.

5. _____ The children needed to row the canoe <u>carefully</u>.

6. _____ The ballet dancer jumped <u>high</u>.

7. _____ I have <u>seven</u> pencils in my desk.

8. _____ That is a <u>funny</u> book!

9. _____ Antoine ordered a <u>healthy</u> smoothie for his snack.

10. _____ Throw me the ball <u>gently</u>.

Review: Adjectives and Adverbs

Circle the letter that identifies the adjective in each sentence.

1. The bluebird flew to the birdbath.

   A. bluebird

   B. flew

   C. the

2. Pretty cardinals also enjoyed the bath.

   A. Pretty

   B. cardinals

   C. enjoyed

Circle the letter that identifies the adverb in each sentence.

3. Two mockingbirds sang beautifully in the trees.

   A. Two

   B. mockingbirds

   C. beautifully

4. The robins ate the worms quickly.

   A. ate

   B. worms

   C. quickly

Review: Parts of Speech

Identify each underlined word by writing *N* for noun, *V* for verb, *ADJ* for adjective, or *ADV* for adverb.

1. _____ The butterfly has a <u>long</u> tube for a tongue.

2. _____ Butterflies <u>go</u> through four stages in their development.

3. _____ The <u>first</u> stage of a butterfly's life is the egg stage.

4. _____ Next is the larval stage, when it is a <u>caterpillar</u>.

5. _____ When it is time, the caterpillar <u>forms</u> a chrysalis.

6. _____ During the fourth stage <u>the</u> butterfly comes out of the chrysalis.

7. _____ Adult butterflies <u>eat</u> many things such as sap, nectar, and the <u>juices</u> of fruits.

8. _____ <u>Butterflies</u> eat by uncoiling their long, tube-like tongues.

9. _____ Sometimes, the colors and patterns of the butterflies' wings <u>help</u> protect them from enemies.

10. _____ Some butterflies have eyespots on their wings that <u>often</u> fool their enemies.

Review: Parts of Speech

Underline each adverb.

1. The red fox ran quickly.

2. Soon, my aunt will arrive.

Circle each noun.

3. Miguel plays for my team.

4. We were not able to play checkers.

Draw a box around each verb.

5. Now, the ball bounced easily.

6. Neyla ran to the store.

Draw a star above each adjective.

7. The happy cats purred quietly.

8. My new dress fits well.

What Is a Sentence?

Write *S* if the group of words is a sentence. Write *NS* if the group of words is not a sentence.

> A **sentence** is a group of words that expresses a complete thought.
>
> Examples: Rupert walked the dog. (sentence)
>
> Walked the dog. (not a sentence)

1. _____ Alex Haley was a writer.

2. _____ Famous for his book.

3. _____ The book.

4. _____ He wrote about an ancestor.

5. _____ His family in New York.

6. _____ Haley wrote historical fiction.

7. _____ Both of Haley's parents were teachers.

8. _____ Really enjoyed his biography of Malcolm X.

9. _____ Haley the special Pulitzer Prize in 1977.

10. _____ He also wrote *Roots: The Saga of an American Family.*

Declarative and Interrogative Sentences

Write **D** if the sentence is a declarative sentence. Write **IN** if the sentence is an interrogative sentence.

A **declarative sentence** makes a statement and ends with a period (**.**).

Example: Joseph ran around the bases. **Declarative**

An **interrogative sentence** asks a question and ends with a question mark (**?**).

Example: Did Joseph run around the bases? **Interrogative**

1. _____ Braden was on my team.

2. _____ Which is your team?

3. _____ Did you see Robert hit the ball?

4. _____ Our team had something to eat after the game.

5. _____ My dog Coco loves to sleep and eat.

6. _____ What time is the movie?

7. _____ Squash is my favorite vegetable.

8. _____ We left an hour ago.

Imperative and Exclamatory Sentences

Write *IM* if the sentence is an imperative sentence. Write *E* if the sentence is an exclamatory sentence.

An **imperative sentence** tells someone to do something and ends with a period (**.**).

Example: Wait until the bus stops. **Imperative**

An **exclamatory sentence** shows strong feeling, such as surprise, fear, or excitement. An exclamatory sentence ends with an exclamation point (**!**).

Example: Wow, that is a huge horse! **Exclamatory**

1. _____ Please, open the screen door.

2. _____ The bus is here!

3. _____ Clean your room.

4. _____ Get the bug spray.

5. _____ Watch out!

6. _____ Please, pass the peas and carrots.

7. _____ Be careful around the hot stove!

8. _____ Run three laps before practice begins.

Subjects in Sentences

Underline the subject in each sentence.

The **subject** of a sentence tells what or whom the sentence is about. The subject can be one word or more than one word.

Example: The grocery store was crowded.

1.   Astronauts are very brave people.

2.   Her birthday is today.

3.   The big, red boat raced across the water.

4.   The crowd enjoyed the fireworks.

5.   Dasha loves to garden.

6.   Our garden produces many vegetables to eat.

7.   Chloe plays basketball at her school.

8.   We had lots of fun this weekend!

Predicates in Sentences

Underline the predicate in each sentence.

> The **predicate** tells what the subject does. The predicate can be one word or more than one word.
>
> Example: About 350 species of birds <u>live in the Grand Canyon.</u>

1. My dogs walk very quickly.

2. Brian's dad drove to the gym.

3. Ms. Nez hung a swing on her porch.

4. We recycle this kind of plastic.

5. This store sells white peaches now.

6. These scraps will go in our compost pile.

7. I enjoyed reading this month's magazine article.

8. We should ride our bikes to the park.

Writing Complete Sentences

Rewrite these incomplete thoughts as complete sentences.

A good writer uses **complete sentences** to make her thoughts clear.

1. smelled the flowers

   _____

2. walked home

   _____

3. the brown bunny

   _____

4. the top shelf

   _____

5. under the stairs

   _____

Writing Sentences

Rewrite each sentence as a different type of sentence.

A good writer uses a variety of sentences including declarative, interrogative, imperative, and exclamatory sentences.

Examples: Fred is helping me. (Declarative)
Is Fred helping me? (Interrogative)
Help me, Fred. (Imperative)
Help me! (Exclamatory)

1. Take the dog on a walk.

_____

_____

2. Dad made a salad.

_____

_____

3. Where is my brown jacket?

_____

_____

4. It is so hot today!

_____

_____

5. The movie is starting soon.

_____

_____

Review: Sentences

Write *D* if the sentence is declarative, *IN* if it is interrogative, *IM* if it is imperative, or *E* if it is exclamatory. Add the correct end punctuation.

1. _____ Who paid to visit the top of the building

2. _____ Please, pay the fee to visit the top of the building

3. _____ Much of the office space remained empty for years

4. _____ This view is amazing

Underline each subject once and each predicate twice.

5. The Empire State Building cost a lot of money to build.

6. The limestone, marble, and steel building took 410 days to complete.

7. The owners depended on sightseers to pay the building's taxes.

8. It is located on Fifth Avenue in New York City.

Capitalizing the First Word in a Sentence

Write the capital letter above each word that should be capitalized.

The first word of every sentence begins with a **capital letter**.

Example: **M**y car has a flat tire.

1. many people think that Jack London is a good American author.

2. he was born in San Francisco, California.

3. while he was young, London spent a lot of time by the waterfront in Oakland, California.

4. london only went to school through grade school.

5. he liked to read and so returned to high school and graduated.

Capitalizing Proper Nouns

Underline and capitalize each proper noun.

A **proper noun** names a specific person, place, or thing. A proper noun begins with a capital letter. Each word in a proper noun begins with a capital letter.

Example: **San Diego** is a city in **California**.

1. My dentist, dr. gladd, takes care of my teeth.

2. My friends jeffrey, john, and ana also go to dr. gladd.

3. I live on peachtree street in atlanta, georgia.

4. december is my favorite month of the year.

5. Our family visited the grand canyon last summer.

6. uncle dion took me to the san diego science center today.

7. We take rover to sunnydale animal hospital on main street.

Capitalizing Place Names

Write the capital letter above each word that should be capitalized.

The important words in **place names** begin with capital letters. The name of a street, a road, a place, a building, or a monument is also capitalized.

Example: Piedmont Hospital is on Pine Valley Road in Austin, Texas.

1. my friend julio hiked near the grand canyon.

2. sean is a nurse at northside healthcare on johnson road.

3. when we were in chicago, we visited lake michigan.

4. the louvre is a famous museum in paris, france.

5. yellowstone, glacier, and yosemite are national parks.

6. the space needle is a landmark in seattle, washington.

Capitalizing Days, Months, and Holidays

Write the capital letter above each word that should be capitalized.

The days of the week, the months of the year, and the names of holidays are **capitalized**.

Examples: **M**onday, **J**uly, **M**other's **D**ay

1. A holiday in january is martin luther king, jr. day.

2. Many nations celebrate united nations day in october.

3. Do you know what happens on groundhog day

   in february?

4. Two holidays in december are christmas and hanukkah.

5. Which day of the week is your favorite: monday,

   wednesday, thursday, or saturday?

6. Our school is closed for summer vacation during june,

   july, and august.

Abbreviations

Write a sentence using each abbreviation.

An **abbreviation** is a shortened form of a word. Most abbreviations begin with a capital letter and end with a period.

1. Tuesday _____

   _____

2. October _____

   _____

3. Avenue _____

   _____

4. Street _____

   _____

5. Doctor _____

   _____

6. Captain _____

   _____

7. February _____

   _____

8. Monday _____

   _____

Abstract

Write the correct abbreviation for each underlined word.

An **abbreviation** is a shortened form of a word. Most abbreviations begin with a capital letter and end with a period.

Examples: **St.**   Street
P.O.   Post Office

Abbreviations for states are special. They are two letters that are capitalized without any periods.

Examples: **GA**   Georgia
VT   Vermont
NY   New York

1. 822 Sherwood <u>Lane</u>

    _____

2. <u>Post Office</u> Box 47825

    _____

3. <u>California</u>

    _____

4. <u>Texas</u>

    _____

5. <u>North Carolina</u>

    _____

6. 6258 Windy <u>Avenue</u>

    _____

7. 612 Orchard <u>Drive</u>

    _____

8. <u>Apartment</u> 210

    _____

Commas in a Series

Add commas where needed.

A **comma** (,) is used to separate words in a series of three or more items. A comma and the word *and* are used before the last item in a series.

Example: Paige danced**,** sang**, and** acted in the play.

1. Amelia planted pansies roses and daisies in her garden.

2. On Tuesday Wednesday and Thursday it rained.

3. Philadelphia Chicago and Atlanta have orchestras.

4. The tourists came from Poland Germany and Italy.

5. Please bring a notebook paper and pencil to class.

6. The five Great Lakes are Lake Erie Lake Huron Lake Michigan Lake Ontario and Lake Superior.

Introductory Words and Phrases

Add commas where needed.

A **comma** (,) follows an introductory word or phrase to separate it from the rest of the sentence.

Examples: **Yes,** I like macaroni and cheese.

Then, I put on my jacket.

A comma also follows the name of a person who is being addressed.

Example: **Jeremy,** show us your new bicycle.

1. First read the directions before beginning.

2. Next study the examples given.

3. Holly have you read the directions?

4. Yes she told the teacher she had read the directions.

5. Jamar wash your hands.

6. Now wait a minute for me to tie my shoes.

Dates, Greetings, and Closings

Add commas where needed.

A **comma** (,) is placed between the date of the month and the year. A comma is also used after the year within a sentence.

Example: On Sunday, August 27, 2010, Andre Taylor was born.

A **comma** (,) is used after the greeting in a friendly letter and after the closing in any letter.

Examples: Dear Uncle Henry,

Sincerely,

July 6 2011

Dear Claire

Thank you for inviting me to your party on July 2 2011. I had a great time, and the games were lots of fun. I will see you when school starts on Monday August 27. Have a good summer!

Yours truly

Chloe

Friendly Letter

Use the words in the word bank to label the parts of this friendly letter.

body	closing	date	greeting	signature

_____ August 21, 2012

Dear Jenna, _____

    How do you like living in Florida? Have you started school yet? I start school next Monday. We have a new principal at our school. Her name is Mrs. Ella Silva. I cannot believe that we will be in the third grade this year! We will learn to write cursive letters and to memorize the multiplication tables. My mother bought me multiplication flash cards and an activities workbook so that I can be ready.

    I wish that you were here to practice and play with me. I hope that you have a great school year. Do not forget to write me a letter soon.

_____ Your friend,

_____ Carla

Quotation Marks

Add quotation marks where needed.

Quotation marks (" ") are written before and after the titles of magazine articles, newspaper articles, songs, and poems. Quotation marks are also written around the chapter titles of a book.

Book titles do not use quotation marks. They are underlined.

Examples: I read "School Gets New Roof" in today's newspaper. (article)

"Dogs, Dogs, Dogs" is my favorite chapter in this book. (chapter)

She sang "Row, Row, Row Your Boat" as she walked. (song)

1. Ian's birds sing along when Robin, Robin plays on the radio.

2. Read How to Be Nice to Your Teacher in this month's magazine.

3. My favorite poem is One Inch Tall by Shel Silverstein.

4. Julie saw the article How to Walk Your Dog in the newspaper.

5. Barrie's favorite song is Twinkle, Twinkle, Little Star.

Quotation Marks

Add quotation marks and ending punctuation where needed.

> A **quotation** is the exact words that someone says. A quotation begins and ends with **quotation marks** (" "). Commas or ending punctuation are placed inside the quotation marks.
>
> Example: Thomas asked, **"Are you going to the shoe store?"**

1.   Marisa asked, Have you read your science lesson

2.   Veronica answered, I read the science lesson last night

3.   Ebony asked, Are you going to the musical this Saturday

4.   Cayce asked, Are we going bowling or are we going skating

5.   Adam responded, Yes, we are going bowling Friday

Review: Punctuation and Capitalization

Circle the sentence that shows the correct punctuation.

1. A. People use reindeer for food, clothing and shelter,

   B. People use reindeer for food clothing and shelter.

   C. People use reindeer for food, clothing, and shelter.

2. A. The baby was born on Aug. 1, 2011, in Boston.

   B. The baby was born on Aug. 1, 2011, in Boston?

   C. The baby was born on Aug. 1, 2011 in Boston

Circle the sentence that shows the correct capitalization.

3. A. Andrew and Melissa rode the school bus.

   B. andrew and Melissa rode the school bus.

   C. Andrew and Melissa rode the School Bus.

4. A. Dr. ahmed and Mrs. Freeman played golf today.

   B. dr. Ahmed and Mrs. freeman played golf today.

   C. Dr. Ahmed and Mrs. Freeman played golf today.

To, Two, and Too

Write the correct form of *to*, *two*, or *too* to complete each sentence.

> The words **to**, **two**, and **too** sound the same, but they are spelled differently and have different meanings. Clues in a sentence tell you which word to use.
>
> Examples: Alex walked **to** the bus stop.
>
>   My cat has **two** kittens.
>
>   Bob played ball, **too**.

1. Our family lives _____ houses from the end of our street.

2. The Zimmermann family has lives near the end of our street, _____ .

3. There are _____ broken bicycles on the playground.

4. Michael and Jennifer went _____ the grocery store after school.

5. Coach Yu made us run _____ laps around the football field.

Their, There, and They're

Write the correct form of *their*, *there*, or *they're* to complete each sentence.

The words *their*, *there*, and *they're* sound the same, but they are spelled differently and have different meanings. Clues in a sentence tell you which word to use.

Examples: **Their** car is brand new.

My dog is sleeping **there**.

They're coming to the party tonight.

1. _____ having a party for Jessica next Saturday.

2. My best friend and I are going _____ .

3. _____ going to play games and roller skate at the party.

4. Lin told me that many friends would be _____ .

5. _____ house will be decorated with yellow balloons and pink streamers.

6. Do you know what _____ party theme will be?

Synonyms

Write a synonym for each underlined word.

Synonyms are words that have the same or almost the same meaning.

Examples:　small　　　little, tiny

　　　　　　big　　　　large, huge

1.　Did you see how <u>speedy</u> the car was?

　　_____

2.　The <u>smelly</u> bug crawled across the driveway.

　　_____

3.　My <u>furry</u> dog barked at the squirrels.

　　_____

4.　Noah was <u>happy</u> to see his grandparents.

　　_____

5.　My teacher is always <u>nice</u> to us.

　　_____

Antonyms

Write an antonym for each underlined word.

Antonyms are words that have opposite meanings.

Examples: big   little

up   down

1. My sister is too <u>tall</u> to ride the roller coaster.

   _____

2. Please, look <u>over</u> the stairs for your suitcase.

   _____

3. Alycia patted the pony's <u>rough</u> coat.

   _____

4. The <u>soft</u> mattress was difficult to sleep on.

   _____

5. Place this box on the <u>top</u> shelf of the closet.

   _____

Scrambled Sentences

Unscramble each group of words to write a complete sentence. Add correct capitalization and punctuation.

1. dogs quickly ran three

    _____

2. fast a flew bird

    _____

3. loudly the clapped crowd

    _____

4. children quickly seven raced

    _____

5. two happily puppies played

    _____

6. beautifully band played the

    _____

7. landed butterfly a gently

    _____

8. five talked noisily students

    _____

Goofy Grammar 1

Write a word for each part of speech below.

1. adjective _____

2. plural noun _____

3. noun _____

4. plural noun _____

5. noun _____

6. adjective _____

7. adjective _____

8. noun _____

9. noun _____

10. verb _____

11. verb _____

12. noun _____

13. verb _____

14. noun _____

15. noun _____

16. noun _____

Goofy Grammar 1

Use the numbered words you wrote on page 72 to complete the passage.

There are two _____ kinds of elephants. One is
                     1

the African elephant, which has large _____ . The
                                 2

African elephant is the largest living land _____ .
                                    3

Both the male and female have _____ . The other
                             4

_____ is the Asian elephant, which has
        5

_____ ears, and only the _____ male
        6   **7**

has _____ .
     8

An elephant's trunk does not have _____ , but
                           9

it does have muscles. It is used to _____ up grass
                             10

and leaves and _____ them to the elephant's
                 11

_____ . The trunk is also used to bring water to the
        12

elephant's mouth or to _____ it on the elephant's
                       13

_____ . Other uses for the trunk include making
        14

trumpet calls, pulling down _____ , and smelling the
                        15

_____ .
     16

Goofy Grammar 2

Write a word for each part of speech below.

1. adjective _____

2. verb _____

3. verb _____

4. verb _____

5. verb _____

6. proper noun _____

7. adjective _____

8. adjective _____

9. adverb _____

10. noun _____

11. adjective _____

12. verb _____

13. noun _____

14. verb _____

15. verb _____

Goofy Grammar 2

Use the numbered words you wrote on page 74 to complete the passage.

Three _____ goldfish _____
            1   2
in the little pond. All day long they would _____
                                          3
and _____ . Sometimes they would even
          4
_____ into the air. The oldest one was named
      5
_____ , and he would be one year old on Friday.
      6
This goldfish was kind of _____ and
                           7
_____ .This meant that the other goldfish acted
      8
_____ towards him. He did not care too much
      9
because he knew that they looked to him for _____ .
                                               10

The middle goldfish was named Fred. He was very

_____ to the others. Fred wanted to be just like
      11
the oldest goldfish. He would follow him around the pond and

_____ just like the older one.
      12

Alden was the youngest goldfish. He wanted to be a

_____ . Because of that he would
      13
_____ all day long. These three goldfish were
      14
the best of friends. They continued to live in the pond and

_____ for their whole lives.
      15

Answer Key

Page 3
1. Raccoons, animals, food, night;
2. North America, kinds, raccoons;
3. raccoon, pounds, kilograms;
4. raccoon, rings, tail, mask, face;
5. Raccoons, areas, woods, water

Page 4
1. Mice, rodents, teeth; 2. Mice, noses, bodies; 3. mice, areas; 4. Mice, plains, deserts; 5. mice, insects; 6. book, mice, rodents; 7. mouse, mouse, world; 8. mouse, house

Page 5
Monday, Oak Street, Katherine, George Washington, Mr. Toma, Piedmont Park, South Dakota, Roberto

Page 6
1. hats; 2. beaches; 3. coats; 4. boxes; 5. trunks

Page 7
1. the class's teacher; 2. the dog's tail; 3. the tree's bark; 4. the girl's skirt; 5. the student's book

Page 8
1. babies'; 2. students'; 3. ships'; 4. grandparents'; 5. dogs'

Page 9
Mammoth Cave, world's, system, Mammoth Cave, part, Mammoth Cave National Park, park, Kentucky, Green River, Nolin River, park, park, 1941, Mammoth Cave, wonders, Western Hemisphere, cave, ridge, limestone, miles (kilometers), walkways, visitors, cave, levels, level, feet (meters), surface, rocks, cave, colors, shapes, lakes, rivers, cave, river, Echo River, width, feet (meters), feet (meters), depth, fish, Echo River, inches (centimeters), types, creatures, Mammoth Cave

Page 10
1. we; 2. I; 3. You, It; 4. They, us; 5. We, him; 6. me; 7. I, her, She; 8. He, them

Page 11
1. she, her; 2. him, he; 3. them, they; 4. her, it; 5. it; 6. she, her; 7. they, them; 8. it; 9. she, he, her; 10. they, them

Page 12
1. I; 2. It; 3. We; 4. They; 5. You; 6. he; 7. She; 8. You, I

Page 13
1. them; 2. me; 3. him; 4. her; 5. them

Page 14
1. My; 2. your; 3. our; 4. yours; 5. Their

Page 15
1. C; 2. A; 3. B; 4. D; 5. A

Page 16
1. pulled; 2. built; 3. carried; 4. help; 5. protect; 6. shows

Page 17
1. do; 2. control; 3. search; 4. explore; 5. give; 6. find, save; 7. need; 8. climb, grab, record

Page 18
1. am; 2. are; 3. are; 4. is; 5. is

Page 19
1. is; 2. are; 3. could; 4. has; 5. will; 6. had; 7. should; 8. will

Page 20
1. use; 2. make; 3. have; 4. swings; 5. traps; 6. are; 7. leaves; 8. need

Answer Key

Page 21
1. traveled; 2. arrived; 3. roamed; 4. sailed; 5. studied

Page 22
1. will write; 2. will study; 3. will sing; 4. will enjoy; 5. will plan; 6. will jump

Page 23
1. ran; 2. saw; 3. come; 4. went; 5. done

Page 24
1. eaten; 2. sang; 3. given; 4. took; 5. began

Page 25
1. can't; 2. haven't; 3. couldn't; 4. weren't; 5. doesn't; 6. shouldn't; 7. didn't; 8. wouldn't

Page 26
1. you'd; 2. he's; 3. it's; 4. she'd; 5. I'm; 6. you're; 7. we'll; 8. they've; 9. she's; 10. I'll

Page 27
1. played; 2. cheered; 3. saw; 4. stops; 5. watched; 6. began; 7. have; 8. wasn't

Page 28
1. C; 2. A; 3. D; 4. C

Page 29
1. stories; 2. he'd; 3. our; 4. made; 5. raccoon; 6. they; 7. will study; 8. me; 9. walk; 10. Paris; 11. is; 12. can't

Page 30
1. loads; 2. ropes; 3. person; 4. papermakers; 5. bags

Page 31
Answers will vary.

Page 32
1. Many; 2. most; 3. several; 4. many; 5. 100; 6. few; 7. six; 8. some

Page 33
1. underground; 2. dried; 3. tiny; 4. good; 5. brave; 6. average; 7. Friendly; 8. famous

Page 34
1. circle: a, underline: doghouse; 2. circle: The, underline: movie; 3. circle: an, underline: umbrella, circle: the, underline: rain; 4. circle: a, underline: leak; 5. circle: the, underline: sun

Page 35
1. smaller; 2. colder; 3. softer; 4. longer; 5. deeper

Page 36
1. longest; 2. shortest; 3. tallest; 4. hardest; 5. longest

Page 37
1. happily; 2. carefully; 3. quickly; 4. gracefully; 5. Suddenly; 6. quietly; 7. patiently; 8. eagerly

Page 38
Answers will vary.

Page 39
1. always; 2. Yesterday; 3. often; 4. today; 5. Now; 6. soon; 7. usually; 8. early

Page 40
1. outside; 2. far; 3. there; 4. forward; 5. close; 6. near; 7. past; 8. through

Page 41
1. circle: quickly, underline: closes; 2. circle: often, underline: plays; 3. circle: tonight, underline: will watch; 4. circle: quietly, underline: worked; 5. circle: yesterday, underline: ran; 6. circle: today, underline: flew; 7. circle: tomorrow, underline: will miss; 8. circle: carefully, underline: mixed;

Answer Key

9. circle: later, underline: will eat;
10. circle: always, underline: stops

Page 42
1. ADV; 2. ADJ; 3. ADV; 4. ADJ;
5. ADV; 6. ADV; 7. ADJ; 8. ADJ;
9. ADJ; 10. ADV

Page 43
1. C; 2. A; 3. C; 4. C

Page 44
1. ADJ; 2. V; 3. ADJ; 4. N; 5. V;
6. ADJ; 7. V; 8. N; 9. V; 10. ADV

Page 45
1. quickly; 2. Soon; 3. Miguel, team;
4. checkers; 5. bounced; 6. ran;
7. The, happy; 8. new

Page 46
1. S; 2. NS; 3. NS; 4. S; 5. NS; 6. S;
7. S; 8. NS; 9. NS; 10. S

Page 47
1. D; 2. IN; 3. IN; 4. D; 5. D; 6. IN;
7. D; 8. D

Page 48
1. IM; 2. E; 3. IM; 4. IM; 5. E; 6. IM;
7. E; 8. IM

Page 49
1. Astronauts; 2. Her birthday;
3. The big, red boat; 4. The crowd;
5. Dasha; 6. Our garden; 7. Chloe;
8. We

Page 50
1. walk very quickly; 2. drove to the
gym; 3. hung a swing on her porch;
4. recycle this kind of plastic; 5. sells
white peaches now; 6. will go in our
compost pile; 7. enjoyed reading this
month's magazine article; 8. should
ride our bikes to the park

Page 51
Answers will vary.

Page 52
Answers will vary.

Page 53
1. IN, ?; 2. IM, .; 3. D, .; 4. E, !;
5. underline once: The Empire State
Building, underline twice: cost a
lot of money to build; 6. underline
once: The limestone, marble, and
steel building, underline twice: took
410 days to complete; 7. underline
once: The owners, underline twice:
depended on sightseers to pay the
building's taxes; 8. underline once:
It, underline twice: is located on Fifth
Avenue in New York City

Page 54
1. Many; 2. He; 3. While; 4. London;
5. He

Page 55
1. Dr. Gladd; 2. Jeffrey, John, Ana,
Dr. Gladd; 3. Peachtree Street,
Atlanta, Georgia; 4. December;
5. Grand Canyon; 6. Uncle Dion,
San Diego Science Center; 7. Rover,
Sunnydale Animal Hospital, Main
Street

Page 56
1. My, Julio, Grand Canyon; 2. Sean,
Northside Healthcare, Johnson Road;
3. When, Chicago, Lake Michigan;
4. The, Louvre, Paris, France;
5. Yellowstone, Glacier, Yosemite;
6. The, Space Needle, Seattle,
Washington

Page 57
1. January, Martin Luther King, Jr.
Day; 2. United Nations Day, October;
3. Groundhog Day, February;
4. December, Christmas, Hanukkah;
5. Monday, Wednesday, Thursday,
Saturday; 6. June, July, August

Answer Key

Page 58
Sentences will vary. 1. Tues.; 2. Oct.;
3. Ave.; 4. St.; 5. Dr.; 6. Capt.; 7. Feb.;
8. Mon.

Page 59
1. Ln.; 2. P.O.; 3. CA; 4. TX; 5. NC;
6. Ave.; 7. Dr.; 8. Apt.

Page 60
1. pansies, roses, and daisies;
2. Tuesday, Wednesday, and
Thursday; 3. Philadelphia, Chicago,
and Atlanta; 4. Poland, Germany,
and Italy; 5. notebook, paper, and
pencil; 6. Lake Erie, Lake Huron, Lake
Michigan, Lake Ontario, and Lake
Superior

Page 61
1. First,; 2. Next,; 3. Holly,; 4. Yes,;
5. Jamar,; 6. Now,

Page 62

July 6, 2011

Dear Claire,
        Thank you for inviting me to
your party on July 2, 2011. I had a
great time, and the games were lots
of fun. I will see you when school
starts on Monday, August 27. Have a
good summer!

Yours truly,
Chloe

Page 63

Date
August 21, 2012

Dear Jenna, **Greeting**

Body
How do you like living in
Florida? Have you started
school yet? I start school
next Monday. We have a
new principal at our school.
Her name is Mrs. Ella Silva.

Body
I cannot believe that we
will be in the third grade
this year! We will learn to
write cursive letters and to
memorize the multiplication
tables. My mother bought
me multiplication flash cards
and an activities workbook
so that I can be ready.
    I wish that you were here
to practice and play with
me. I hope that you have a
great school year. Do not
forget to write me a letter
soon.

Closing
Your friend,

Signature
Carla

Page 64
1. "Robin, Robin"; 2. "How to Be
Nice to Your Teacher"; 3. "One Inch
Tall"; 4. "How to Walk Your Dog";
5. "Twinkle, Twinkle, Little Star"

Page 65
1. "Have you read your science
lesson?"; 2. "I read the science
lesson last night."; 3. "Are you going
to the musical this Saturday?";
4. "Are we going bowling or are
we going skating?"; 5. "Yes, we are
going bowling Friday."

Page 66
1. C; 2. A; 3. A; 4. C

Page 67
1. two; 2. too; 3. two; 4. to; 5. two

Page 68
1. They're; 2. there; 3. They're;
4. there; 5. Their; 6. their

Answer Key

Page 69
Answers will vary but may include:
1. fast; 2. stinky; 3. hairy; 4. excited;
5. kind

Page 70
Answers will vary but may include:
1. short; 2. under; 3. smooth; 4. hard;
5. bottom

Page 71
Answers will vary but may include:
1. Three dogs ran quickly.; 2. A bird
flew fast.; 3. The crowd clapped
loudly.; 4. Seven children raced
quickly.; 5. Two puppies played
happily.; 6. The band played
beautifully.; 7. A butterfly landed
gently.; 8. Five students talked
noisily.

Pages 72–75
Answers will vary.